THE WAY TO FINANCIAL FREEDOM

Proven path to personal finance and wealthy living.

Bill Walter

All rights reserved. No part of this publication may be reproduced, distributed, or transmitted in any form or by any means, including photocopying, recording, or other electronic or mechanical methods, without the prior written permission of the publisher, except in the case of brief quotations embodied in critical reviews and certain other noncommercial uses permitted by copyright law.

Copyright©Bill Walter, 2022.

TABLE OF CONTENT

CHAPTER 1

CHAPTER 2

CHAPTER 3

CHAPTER 4

CHAPTER 5

INTRODUCTION

Financial independence implies various things to different individuals. For others, it implies having the capacity to manage unforeseen bills or crises. For others, financial independence means paying cash for a significant purchase, such as a new automobile or a dream trip.

Maybe your definition of financial independence is knowing that you can retire when you're ready, on your terms, and enjoy the lifestyle you desire.

Whatever your exact idea of financial independence is, what it ultimately comes down to is you having control over your money, instead of the other way around.

CHAPTER 1
WHAT YOU CAN DO TO CONTROL YOUR MONEY

As with most new undertakings, getting started is one of the toughest aspects of the process. To help you start your financial freedom path, let's go over a few of the most efficient, time-tested ways for cutting expenditures, regulating spending, and setting you up for financial independence.

1. Track your expenditures so you know where your money is going.
Keeping a journal of your everyday expenditures is an excellent first step toward financial independence. Many individuals spend blindly on needless items and services, then wonder why they never have any spare income.

Tracking your spending patterns over time helps you find and reduce needless purchases. For example, $4 a day for your morning coffee may not seem like a lot at the moment, but for a year, those coffees add up to more than $933. That's money that might be accumulating interest in your IRA.

To get started, take an inventory of your spending patterns. Look through your bank account and your credit card bills and note all of your transactions over the last six months. Then classify all of your purchases by kind. Some of your costs will be fixed, such as your mortgage, auto insurance, and energy payments. Others are more changeable, including grocery store expenditures, odd shoe splurges, and that magazine subscription you forget you had.

Tracking your expenditure doesn't have to be complex. A basic spreadsheet or personal cost-tracking software is all you need. Once you have your costs input and classified, you can see where your money goes each month and make educated judgments about where to cut spending.

2. Set a budget (and stick to it).

Now that you have the general picture of which costs are important and which may be removed or decreased, you can start on a budget. Although budgeting may not seem like a lot of fun, if you stick with it, the ultimate result will make it all worthwhile.

It's vital to remember that making a budget is more than declaring, "I will only spend X amount this month." Budgeting involves discipline and another one of those spreadsheets or budgeting software.

Referring back to your trimmed-down spending inventory, compare your revenue to your outflow. If there isn't anything left over after the bills is paid, you'll need to seek for additional expenditures to decrease. Don't be scared to be ruthless and trim down to only the basics; this is just temporary. You can live with one streaming service instead of three, and most retail brands are just as excellent as the pricey ones.

Once you have your budget established, the problem becomes adhering to it. It takes a lot of determination to quit the wasteful spending habit. Find an accountability partner to be your support system and ask them to remind you of your objectives when you are trying to avoid a nonessential buy.
Track your spending patterns and take control of your budget with our free Budget Worksheet.

3. Plan how to pay off your debt.

A lot of individuals describe financial freedom as being free from their debt. Although purchasing a home might be challenging without a mortgage, we can start with something more feasible such as removing credit card debt and even auto loans. Your tiny moves towards financial independence nevertheless influence your overall health finances. Some money gurus advocate paying off your debt with the lowest sum initially so we can generate momentum and enthusiasm.

It is vital to keep in mind that when you do pay off that debt, don't put the money you had been paying your debt into your budget. Instead, take the cash and apply it to the next obligation you're attempting to pay off.

4. Create an emergency fund—start small and dream large.

Studies demonstrate that for many U.S. homes, an unexpected $400 spend would damage their capacity to meet their usual monthly expenses. Without funds to pay for a medical emergency, auto repair, or a broken appliance, frequently the only choice is to use a credit card. This adds even more debt that must be repaid before you can reach financial independence.

The greatest approach to avoid one of life's curveballs from derailing your financial ambitions is to construct an emergency fund. Initially, you may assume you can't afford to save money until you have [insert your hurdle here]. But the fact is you can't afford to have an emergency fund if you desire financial independence.

Ideally, you will have 4-6 months' worth of living costs in your emergency fund. But that's an end goal, not a starting point. Saving even $10 a month is better than saving nothing, so look at your cost monitoring and budget and find a method to designate money to your emergency fund.

Having an emergency fund is so vital to financial freedom that you may even consider finding a means to add to your income, even temporarily. Additional money from a second job, side gig, or even sales of household goods may be directed to your emergency fund, lowering the possibility that an unanticipated cost would considerably add to your debt burden.

5. Don't extend your expenditure to meet your wage rises.

Many individuals make the mistake of raising their lifestyle and spending as their earning ability improves. However, financial independence doesn't equal freedom to spend every dollar you make. In reality, the reverse is true.

If you are devoted to financial independence, how you deploy pay rises or other revenue increases may make a major difference in how fast you reach your objectives.

Instead of investing your additional money on a larger home, a better automobile, or the newest and most costly technology equipment, maintain your present expenses of living. Use your additional income to pay off a credit card, establish a retirement account, or construct a financial safety net in your emergency savings account.

Resisting the impulse to spend every dollar you earn now is a major step toward future financial independence, which is worth much more than the newest smartphone.

How Do You Know When You Have Achieved Financial Freedom?

There is no physical finish line for your financial emancipation quest. Just like establishing the idea, everyone will have their metrics for success.
However, there are a few commonly regarded markers that you are well on your path to obtaining financial freedom:

Limited use of debt for significant purchases, including vehicles

No more living paycheck to paycheck

Over 6 months of spending in an emergency fund safety net

Ability to fund both savings and retirement accounts

Retirement preparedness on your terms.

6. Invest in Financial education.

Investing in Financial education is a vital step in your route to financial freedom. Reading this article is the start of becoming financially educated. The more you study financials, the simpler it is to make sensible financial choices. There is a lot of stuff on the internet that may supply you with knowledge, including this website. It features podcasts, free financial eBooks, and Financial experts eager to assist you with your search for financial independence.

7. Appoint a family financial officer.

You may skip this step if you're single. Households require a designated family financial officer. This family member doesn't make the family's financial choices but rather the one monitoring the success the family has in obtaining financial independence and distributes the progress reports to the rest of the family. After you've designated the family finance officer, arrange a weekly financial date with your spouse. Not only can it benefit the family's financial health but can also be fantastic quality bonding time with your spouse. During these weekly updates, you may discuss your progress toward financial independence, create a strategy to tackle problems and celebrate your achievements over coffee or a wonderful romantic supper.

8. Open different accounts.

Ensure that you establish enough money and choose the suitable account for your financial objectives by splitting them into multiple bank accounts. For your consumable income, the money you spend for your everyday transactions such as shopping, food allowance, and transportation allowance you may place into a transaction account. While cash for your savings may be deposited into a savings/deposit account. This account earns interest if you meet the minimum balance necessary to earn interest. The optimal account for retirement savings is a term deposit account. It needs your money to be kept in the account for a specified length of time. Interest is paid throughout the account's maturity date.

Meanwhile, you should consider isolating your emergency cash from your other accounts to prevent spending it on non-essential purchases.

Here's a cash flow framework to aid you.

The route to financial independence might be simpler when you monitor your income flow correctly.

To better understand cash flow, you may check this "How to combine costly debts and boost cash flow" article.

.

9 . Save first and spend what is left.

"Work increases to occupy the time available for its completion."

-Parkinson's law

Parkinson's rule for time management, in a nutshell, states that if you allow yourself a week to do a simple activity, it will be tougher to finish and you'll end up taking a week to complete it. Some of you may know Parkinson's law applies to time management but I'm here to tell you that it applies to everything, including your money.

How?

Every month you always pledge to yourself that you're going to save a portion of your income. However, you notice yourself spending on things you didn't plan– a sale, retail therapy, and so on, and get up spending what's left on your expenses at the end of the month.

"Do not save what is left after spending, but spend what is left after saving."

-Warren Buffet

Or simply the notion of "save first and consume what is left."

You must be weary of paying your final payment just to find out that you have a few sums remaining. If you're wondering what you can do to end this cycle of earning and losing, we have the appropriate strategy for you. It's termed the "save first and spend what is left." philosophy, the exact opposite of what you've been doing. Calculate your income and expenditures you have and the amount you should be able to save. If you do it well, it will have a big influence on your overall financial health.

10. Prepare to leave your legacy.

This third phase doesn't have much to do with your goal of financial independence, it's all about who are the heirs of the money you will be leaving behind. Create a testament to making sure that your money that was gained by a lifetime of managing money wisely gets up to the appropriate hands, your heirs.

Ensure that money you've worked hard to create goes to the appropriate hands: Estate Planning and Commercial

CHAPTER 2
USE MONEY TO MAKE MONEY

If you're savvy, you can transform one thousand dollars into even more money. Here's how to earn money on investments, even tiny ones.

While there are many ways you may make money quickly by performing odd internet jobs or producing it via things like affiliate marketing or email marketing, to truly generate money by investing with only $1,000 could bring more hurdles, and frankly, greater dangers. That is, of course, unless you know what you're doing.

However, all hazards aside, even if you're living paycheck-to-paycheck, you still may be able to conjure up an additional $1,000 to put towards your investment portfolio if you're imaginative.

Before you start investing, there are basic mentality concepts that you need to stick to. Moving beyond the scarcity mindset is key. Too many of us spend our lives with the belief that there's never enough stuff to go around — that we don't have enough time, financial flow, relationships, or opportunity to develop and experience life at a higher level.

That's simply a belief system. Think and you will become. If you believe you can't become wealthy or even create a large quantity of additional passive income by putting it into successful short-term investment goals, then it's far more of a mentality problem than anything else. You don't need to invest a lot of money using any of the following tactics to attain your financial objectives.

Sure, having more money to invest would be wonderful. But it's not essential. As long as you can discover the proper method that works for you, all you need to do is scale. It's analogous to establishing an offer online, discovering the optimum conversion rate via optimization, then growing it out. If you know you can invest $1 and earn two dollars, you'll continue to invest a dollar.

Start small. Try alternative techniques. Track and evaluate your findings. Don't get too hooked up on how you're going to become insanely wealthy overnight. That won't happen. But if you can leverage one of the following strategies to create a little money by investing modest, brief bursts of cash, then all you have to do is scale — plain and easy. You don't have to overthink things.

How to invest $1,000 to earn money quickly
If you have $1,000 to invest, you may generate fast money in some ways. But there are certain approaches that top others. The play here is speed. We're not talking about long-term, buy-hold tactics. Those are fantastic if you're trying to invest your cash

over at least a two- to five-year timeframe. We're talking about methods you can generate money quickly.

Even when it comes to markets that could take time to move or have longer cycles, investments can frequently result in actual profits and rapid returns by using the proper tactics. So what's the best investing strategy? Sure, long-term works. Real estate and other time-intensive tactics will ultimately bring you there.

Raghee Horner of Simpler Futures thinks that "long-term interest rates are the next big trade," but Jim Cramer of Mad Money argues that "there are loads of individuals who are late to trends by nature and embrace a trend when it's no longer in vogue." By hopping in and out of long-term investments like that, you're much more likely to lose your shirt than if you time your short-term bets exactly perfectly.

It's not so much about trying to catch the next trend. It's not about being a webinar genius like Liz Benny — or even setting your sales funnels or improving your conversions. Investing your money is more about paying close attention to indications that may truly shift the needle in the near term as opposed to the longer term. It's also about leveraging and properly hedging your assets without putting too much risk tolerance on the line.

That doesn't imply that you don't need a long-term plan. You surely do. But if you're wanting to build some momentum and earn some cash rapidly, in the short future, then the following investing tips could help you achieve exactly that.

1. Trade in the stock market.

Day trading is not for the faint of heart. It needs tenacity and drive. It needs to understand the numerous market factors at play. This isn't anything a stock adviser would advocate for novices. But, if learned and learned effectively, it is a technique where you may fast — within hours — generate a big quantity of actual money with a very minimal investment.

There are additional strategies to hedge your bets when it comes to playing the stock market. Whether you play the general market or trade penny stocks, ensure that you establish stop-loss limits to reduce any possibility for big depreciations. Now, if you're an accomplished trader, you undoubtedly recognize that market makers typically move stocks to play into either our fear of failure or our greed. And they'll frequently drive an individual stock down to a specific price to accentuate that anxiety and play directly into their wallets.

When it comes to penny stocks, this is further amplified. So you have to comprehend what you're doing and be able to assess the market dynamics and achieve large asset appreciation profits. Pay attention to moving averages. Often, when equities break over 200-day moving averages, there's potential for either a major upside or a big fall.

2. Invest in a money-making course.

Investing in yourself is one of the finest conceivable investments you can make. While you may not be able to specify an actualized return on investment, no money's better invested. Invest in yourself. Invest in your education. Learn. Adapt. Grow. Discover what you're enthusiastic about.

There are thousands of money-making courses on the internet. The tricky part is picking the perfect online course for you. From ebooks to affiliate marketing, search engine optimization, and beyond, the opportunities are unlimited. While numerous money-making experts could come up on social media, not all courses are built similarly. Spend time performing your due diligence and studying to find the one that's suitable for you.

3. Trade commodities.

Trading commodities like gold and silver provide a unique opportunity, particularly when they're trading near the lower end of their five-year range. Metrics like those offer a solid indication of where commodities could be going. Carolyn Boroden of Fibonacci Queen adds, "I have long-term support and timing in the silver markets because silver is a strong hedge against inflation. Plus, metals like silver are physical investments that consumers can cling onto."

The basics of economics influence the price of commodities. As supply decreases, demand grows and prices rise. Any interruption to a supply chain hurts pricing. For example, a health concern to animals may substantially affect prices as scarcity reins loss. However, cattle and meat are simply one sort of commodity.

Metals, energy, and agriculture are other types of commodities. To invest, you can use an exchange like the London Metal Exchange or the Chicago Mercantile Exchange, as well as many others. Often, investing in commodities implies investing in futures contracts. Effectively, that's a pre-arranged agreement to acquire a specified amount at a given price in the future. These are leveraged contracts, bringing both great gain and a possibility for a severe downside, so exercise caution.

4. Trade cryptocurrencies.

Cryptocurrencies are on the rise. While trading them could seem hazardous, if you hedge your bets here as well, you might reduce the repercussions from a poorly-timed transaction. There are numerous platforms for trading bitcoins as well. But before you dig in, educate yourself. Find classes on sites like Udemy, Kajabi, or Teachable. And understand the subtleties of trading items like Bitcoin, Ether, Litecoin, and others.

While there are over 3,000 cryptocurrencies in circulation, only a few genuinely matter today. Find an exchange, examine the trading patterns, watch for breakouts of long-term moving averages and get active trading. You may utilize exchanges like Coinbase, Kraken, or Cex.io, along with many others, to do real transactions.

5. Use peer-to-peer lending.

Peer-to-peer lending is a fashionable investing technique these days. While you may not become wealthy investing in a peer-to-peer lending network, you might surely earn a little currency. Which loan platform do you use? Today, there are numerous to pick from, but the most prominent ones are Lending Club, Peer Form, and Prosper.

How does this work? Peer-to-peer lending services enable you to loan tiny bursts of funds to firms or people while receiving an interest rate on the return. You receive more money than you would if you deposited it in a savings account, and your investment risk is minimized since the algorithms are doing most of the hard work for you.

Once you discover the offer, you may delve in and conduct some research — then, you can either accept the bargain or not. You'll have your risk appraised based on a proprietary algorithm that incorporates job and credit history, and you'll be able to choose to invest based on a range of well-thought-out facts.

6. Trade options.

There are loads of vehicles, such as forex and stocks. The ideal strategy to make excellent money by investing when it comes to options is to get in approximately 15 days before corporate results are revealed. What kind should you buy? Money calls.

The ideal moment to sell those money calls is the day before the firm discloses its results. There's simply so much excitement and expectation surrounding results that it often pushes up the price, providing you with a recurring winner. But don't hold through the profits. That's a bet you don't want to take if you're not a seasoned investor, says John Carter from Simpler Trading.

7. Flip real estate contracts.
Making money with real estate can seem like a long-term goal, but it's not. There are methods you can take as little as $500 to $1,000 and utilize the cash invested to flip real estate contracts to generate rapid

money. How? Use a strategy like Kent Clothier's REWW to first learn how the market operates. It'll then give you the data and resources to find unoccupied houses, distressed sellers, and cash buyers.

While most people assume that real estate is won by flipping conventional properties and performing the repairs yourself, the quickest money you can earn in real estate is flipping the actual contract itself. It's arbitrage. Identify motivated sellers and cash buyers, put them together, and efficiently broker the sale. It can seem unusual on the first attempt, but if you get the hang of it, you can become a mini-mogul in the real estate sector by just expanding out this one single method. It works, and it's advocated by some of the world's most successful real estate investors.

CHAPTER 3
HOW TO MANAGE RISK

The risk management method helps you prepare for and anticipate hazards, and mitigation techniques will provide you with skills to deal with them if they do materialize.

Risk Management Method

The risk management method, or lifecycle, is an organized technique for handling hazards that might arise in your project. Though you'll find some modest variance, the risk management process, or lifecycle, usually follows the following phases. This approach may be utilized for both positive and negative risks.

1. Identify hazards

The first step to having a handle on possible dangers is to recognize what they are. In this stage, you'll identify particular hazards that can harm your project by producing a list (or spreadsheet) of risks that might develop. Examples of frequent project hazards include deploying a new technology program for the project, having a poorly defined project aim or deliverable, and not having enough safeguards to protect the health and safety of project team members.

Use your project management knowledge and review comparable historical initiatives to identify what problems you could foresee. You'll also want to have stakeholders, team members, and subject matter experts produce ideas alongside you; they may have insight into the area that you've neglected.

2. Analyze possible risk effect

In the risk analysis step, you'll analyze the possibility of each risk happening, as well as the possible effect each risk will have on your project. You may begin placing this list of hazards in a risk register—a chart that sets out each risk, followed by information like priority level and mitigation methods. You may capture both qualitative and quantitative information.

3. Assign priority to hazards

In this step, you'll give priority to risks by utilizing the likelihood and effect of each risk to define their risk levels. This implies giving each risk a high, medium, or low priority depending on the variables you've established. Evaluating your risks provides your team the ability to determine where to spend their work in decreasing risk.

4. Mitigate hazards

Come up with a strategy to minimize each risk. We'll delve into how you can address hazards in greater depth below. Record these plans in your risk register as well.

5. Monitor hazards

In the final phase, put up a mechanism to monitor each risk as your project starts. You may achieve this by assigning team members to keep an eye on certain risks and minimize them. This makes sure you'll have a continual understanding of where the dangers are and how likely they are to arise, so you'll be ready to face them if they do occur.

Risk Mitigation

The method of coping with hazards
The risk management method offers forth a way for you to deal with hazards before they happen. But what are the practical ways you

may lessen them? Avoid, accept, minimize, and transfer are four basic approaches to limit risk. Deciding which step to apply for each danger isn't an exact science, and you'll have to use your discretion and skills to choose which is best. Here's some extra information and suggestions on each mitigation technique.

1. Avoid

Not all dangers can be avoided, but it might be a good idea to do so when you can. Avoid a risk if there is a high likelihood that danger will happen. Has a partner vendor established a reputation for offering low-quality work? Try to locate a different one. Are you event-planning during the wet season? Move the function inside, or to a sunny season.

2. Accept

Accepting risks might make sense if they have a low possibility of occurring and will have a modest effect on your project. Ultimately if the danger does arise, it shouldn't stop your project. Say you've ordered sunflower arrangements for a wedding reception, but the florist says there's a tiny risk they won't have enough and will have to substitute some with tulips. Since the possibility of danger is minimal and having tulips instead of sunflowers won't upend the wedding, you could take the risk instead of worrying to locate a new florist.

3. Reduce

Reducing risk includes altering items in your strategy to lessen the risk's likelihood of occurring or possible effect on your project. Medium and high risks are strong candidates to attempt to decrease. Reducing normally needs some work or money. For example, a project manager might employ additional team members if the team is lagging on tasks.

This may also entail adding risk-reduction techniques to your project strategy. Time buffers for difficult or time-sensitive jobs might provide you some flexibility if work begins to fall behind. Having a contingency budget may assist absorb unexpected expenditures if they materialize.

4. Transfer

Transferring risks implies moving the risk to another entity outside of your project. This might include buying insurance coverage, or outsourcing portions of the task to a third party. The risk could still exist, but the immediate damage to your project will be absorbed by somebody outside of your project.

Risk management is an essential aspect of project management since the risk is virtually inherent in each project. Don't worry—it's unusual to ever entirely remove the danger. Listen to Stanton, a program manager at YouTube, speak about his experience managing risk throughout his career in the video below.

CHAPTER 4

HOW TO PROTECT YOURSELF ONLINE

With data leaks being disclosed at an alarming pace, it's crucial to take stock of how you safeguard your identity online. In your offline life, you're cautious to shred crucial papers and make sure that not everything gets in the typical rubbish. So why do so many individuals believe it's alright to keep their desktops and mobile devices plugged into online banking accounts? You must be vigilant about safeguarding the information that's vital to you. Here are some strategies to safeguard yourself online.

1. Be cautious about what you disclose

You wouldn't trust just anybody with your personal financial information, or the key code to your home, right? Treat your online information with the same degree of security, which includes storing it in a safe area and not scrawled in a notepad beside your computer, or stored elsewhere in your email account or on your phone. If you must share a password with someone do not provide it via email.

2. Trade only with secured platforms

Before you buy anything on a website, confirm that the website's URL begins with "https://." The "s" at the end is crucial since it shows that your connection is encrypted. Don't buy anything from a website that doesn't contain this. Also, you should think hard about preserving your financial information on websites you purchase from, even if you shop with them regularly. Storing your information on their site might make it simpler for hackers to access it if the company's website or network experiences a data breach.

3. Change your passwords often

It might be a headache to have to remember a whole new set of passwords, but you'll be glad when your accounts stay safe.

Don't use the same passwords for several sites.

Websites appear to be hacked practically every day, which means you'll want to safeguard yourself as much as possible with strong passwords. If you're using the same password for your email, online banking, and social networking sites you're leaving yourself vulnerable to attackers accessing several areas with one piece of information.

4. Watch out for questionable connections

I know this sounds like a simple one, but every day there's a new technique to persuade you to click on a link you don't recognize from a supposedly credible source. And those masterminding these plots are growing savvy, designing sites that appear more and more like a true resource. If you're uncertain about a message or its contents contact the sender to check that the link is acceptable to click.

5. Lock it up

When you're done using your mobile device, computer, or tablet, lock it. Better still, have a password in place. While a 4-digit number on your iPhone isn't infallible, it will nonetheless act as a barrier between your information and the outside world.

6. Make sure your gadgets are up to date

Updates frequently contain essential patches for any security flaws that may have been found in your applications or devices.

7. Use two-factor authentication

Two-factor authentication needs you to authenticate your identity once you've signed in using your login and password. In certain situations, you'll be asked to verify your identity by entering a code delivered by text to your phone or by email. Other times, you'll have to answer a security question.

Whenever two-factor authentication is offered, opt-in. It may take you a few more seconds to log in to your accounts, but it may make it less likely that other people will be able to access your accounts, too.

8. Avoid using insecure public Wi-Fi

If feasible, try to avoid using unprotected public Wi-Fi on your devices. Using it might put you subject to exploitative acts. And if you must use it, avoid inputting sensitive information, such as your Social Security number or bank information, on any websites. Better better, use a VPN, or virtual private network, to perform your surfing while you're not at home. This will encrypt the data you transmit and receive, making it much tougher to intercept.

9. Backup your files frequently

If you become a victim of malware, such as ransomware, you may not be able to get your data back. That is unless you've backed up your data.

When you back up your data, you may make some sorts of security breaches less onerous. If a hacker encrypts your data and demands a ransom to unencrypt it, it's not going to be that big of a concern if you backed it up a week ago.

10. Educate your family

You may be taking all the correct safeguards on your home security network, but if your family and other people utilizing your network aren't doing their bit to keep things secure, your efforts might not be enough.

Make sure that everyone who frequently uses your network understands how to help maintain it safe. Kids can learn about online safety, too.

CHAPTER 5

DIFFERENCE BETWEEN INVESTMENT AND SPECULATION

What is investment

Investment includes the acquisition of assets or security anticipating it will create income or be projected to appreciate in the future. Financial investments include the acquisition of bonds or equities, mutual funds, etc. the term investment is not just restricted to the business sphere; it can be used in personal life as well.

Investments make sure earned money is productive and it being productive is the main part of the financial aspect. Investments are split into fixed income where the rate of return is pre-stated (bonds, preference shares), and variable income where the rate of return is not predetermined (equity shares, etc) (equity shares, etc.)

Some of the classic investments include gold and jewelry, provident funds, term deposits, etc. while some of the alternative investments are antique collections, structured products, private equity investments, etc.

Traditional Investment
Stocks
Bonds
Fixed Deposits
Provident Funds
Gold and Jewellery

Alternative Investment
Real Estate\sPrivate Equity Investments
Antique Collectibles
Paintings
Hedge Fund Investments
Structured Products

Investment is one of the most crucial components of financial planning to guarantee that the money produced is not useless. Today's money will not have the same worth of five years separate from the intrinsic value. Hence, conserving money alone will not be adequate for reaching future financial objectives. Some of the most essential motivations for an investment of money are:

Investing in many financial outlets enables money growth instead of lingering in the bank account with relatively small returns.
The yield returns assist take care of situations such as Medical expenditures etc.
For personal investment, the whole family's future may be safeguarded, such as the schooling and marriage expenditures of children.
Tax minimization is an extra advantage for governments globally to give incentives to people and organizations for making

investments, notably if they are affiliated with the Government or Government-backed institutions.

Inflation may be effectively dealt with. Inflation will keep growing, and savings returns may not necessarily be adequate. The value linked with the volume of money depreciates with growing inflation. The effect of inflation in lowering the value of assets may be managed by investing and creating returns on the corpus.

It is an appealing means of producing money from acquired capital. E.g., rent generated from a real estate investment or equities that have been acquired.

What is Speculation?

This is when investors spend their money speculating in an attempt to generate additional profits from price swings in the market. Life of speculation is short..

Speculation implies a considerably greater degree of risk and more unpredictability of returns while it may be on the same lines as an investor. These speculators are often schooled and take action when the game of probability is strong in their favor. They are quite proud of their views and consider putting a high price. Decisions are considered when the environment is of Panic, Confusion, or high levels of optimism yet still go against the flow.

The possibility of the opposite condition is rare to materialize, but the speculators\s may gain a big sum from that if it does. E.g., if the stock market is going through a bullish period, and the situation is hopeful, the possibilities of collapse are comparatively minimal. Still, speculators might foresee a bearish phase to approach shortly and make their bets appropriately. If the bearish\s phase does materialize, speculators win a significant margin as they made a prediction when bets were against their view.

Many may perceive speculators as hazardous gamblers but they give the much-required liquidity in the market, which is vital for efficiency. In some areas such as commodities, speculators generate considerable liquidity. The only participants would be the Food businesses and the farmers, who may have limited capacity to invest and take the risk.
The bid-ask spread would be broader with smaller players, and it would be difficult to identify a counterpart in case of trade closure. The consequent illiquidity will greatly raise the risk in the market and give a chance to profit more, where the speculator's cash in.

The sale of properties that followed characterizes a condition of a speculative market. The lending rates were low, and speculators were counting on property values continuing to climb as more people would acquire homes (with the assistance of leverage) to sell them when prices rose further at large profits. Speculation may also boost short-term volatility and risk, hence increasing prices and contributing to asset bubbles.

Critical Differences Between Investment and Speculation

An investment involves an asset to achieve returns above the original amount in the future. On the other hand, speculating includes performing a hazardous financial transaction to achieve large-scale profits from a single transaction.

Investments are frequently kept for a lengthy duration, usually more than a year. Instances like real estate and life insurance are kept for 25-30 years. Speculation is kept for a little time, generally less than a year, and may even be on an upcoming event.

The degree of risk taken is generally modest as compared to speculating. Speculation will concentrate on achieving big returns in a comparatively shorter length of time, and therefore, the quantum of risk is quite high. Since investment is usually made by the middle class working for the community, they would be putting the extra money off their hard labor, which they anticipate to receive a reliable return. They are willing to part with their money provided it gives a solid return.

An investor will be utilizing their cash for investing, whilst speculators would utilize borrowed funds and tempt the borrowers with appealing returns.

The aforementioned remark also represents the mentality of the investors and speculators. Investors will typically adopt a cautious and conservative strategy when analyzing the investment and the risk appetite\s they can handle. Speculators believe in an aggressive strategy stressing assault yet a casual attitude. As the profits are simply too enticing, and the window of opportunity is quite limited, this behavior will readily be mirrored.

Investors anticipate benefiting from the change in the value of an asset, while speculators concentrate on extracting gains from price variations due to demand and supply dynamics.

While making judgments, investors will undertake comprehensive research and concentrate on the basic characteristics of the firm, such as the financial condition, ratio analytics, etc. In contrast, speculative judgments are based on technical charts, market dynamics and personal opinions/tips obtained.

The options for contemplating investment will center on the Blue chip companies of the stock market, savings bank accounts, provident funds, etc. Still, speculators will concentrate on the commodities market, options trading, betting, etc.

Investment does not give rise to tactics such as insider trading\s or probable leaking of information, which may be witnessed in speculative activities as their rewards are substantial.

The amount of patience and sacrifice is relatively great in the case of investment but not in the case of speculation. However, the likelihood of losses does grow in speculative activity.

Investment activities are reported separately in a company's balance sheet of a business but speculation is not documented separately. Depending on the returns that they give, such activity may either be categorized under investment or the category of 'Other Assets / Miscellaneous Income.'

The quantity of money for investment activities is comparatively smaller and relies on the competence of the individual/organization while speculating demands huge amounts for performing the activities.

Note: One should not combine speculation with gambling. Both these expressions will frequently be used interchangeably, creating an impression that it implies the same, however, it is not. Gambling includes putting in money on an event that has an unknown conclusion in hopes of gaining more money without any calculation. It is essentially a game of chance with the odds, not necessarily with the gambler.

For instance, a gambler will explore an American roulette game rather than speculate in the commodities market. However, the payoff is just 35 to 1, while the chances of winning are 37 to 1.

Conclusion
One should recognize that all investments involve speculation, but all speculations are not necessarily investments. Both aims are to produce profits; only the approach includes a difference. There is nothing proper or bad in the method, but it relies on

the long-term aim of the person and the degree of risk they are ready to accept.

The fact of the situation is that every task we conduct involves supposition. The person appears in the open and utilizes their judgment to anticipate the future course of events and act appropriately. This unusual mentality leads many investors to shun particular stocks or bonds owing to their unknown potential, making investors gauge safety by the yield and stability supplied. If security is paying over a specific level, it is considered as 'speculative' and not for them.

Hence, one should be aware of the advantages and drawbacks of both these scenarios and retain awareness before arriving at any conclusion and not merely as an Investment or speculative activity. The factor of gambling should also not be overlooked totally, and knowledge of the same should be kept in mind before arriving at any conclusion.

Investing in speculation is an art, not all individuals do it since it demands deep market knowledge and sufficient training. Depending on industry risk and unpredictability of market fluctuations fluctuate.

www.ingramcontent.com/pod-product-compliance
Lightning Source LLC
Chambersburg PA
CBHW050311220526
45465CB00005B/1941